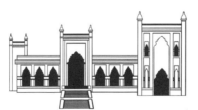

Brand Library & Art Center
1601 West Mountain Street
Glendale, CA 91201
(818) 548-2051
www.brandlibrary.org

JEAN-MARIE MASSAUD

daab

Design is nothing. Life is everything.

As a kid Jean-Marie Massaud wanted to be an inventor – a dream which he turned into reality. These days his aim is not to create utopia but to construct a human vision of sustainable development in the service of life itself. Invention in order to bring form to thought. Constructing to give life substance.

Massaud's central idea is a symbiosis between "culture" and "nature", between "technosphere" and "ecosphere", between man and his environment. He is trying to identify man's relationship with his environment not only through spectacular buildings but also through everyday objects. His involvement in urban design brought about the close linkage between design and architecture and their impact on man and the environment. "To create architecture could be deemed synonymous with creating ecosystems."

Massaud favours an alternative approach to consumption. According to the motto "not more, but better" he aims at improving our quality of life and our experiences.

A market economy is based on growth. There is an urgent need for quantitative growth to mutate into qualitative growth as the earth itself is a finite system.

Objects are nothing but words which enable us to write sentences, stories, to create our environment. Therefore they have to convey both emotional as well as sensual content.

As he sees it, the function of the designer in our lost society can no longer be confined to that of a naïve or cynical stylist, it must expand to that of a scenarist of our environment. Massaud understands the designer as a conscientious catalyst of the aims of his/her era who is responsible for putting forward alternative models of sensible consumption. Convinced as he is that man by nature has to reinvent himself, has to define his individual and collective project of life as a reality, Jean-Marie Massaud believes his work is both committed and resolutely political. "Progress will either be human or not at all."

Design is nothing. Life is everything.

Als Kind wollte Jean-Marie Massaud Erfinder werden. Diesen Wunsch setzte er in die Realität um. Heute geht es ihm nicht darum Utopien, sondern eine menschliche Vision des nachhaltigen Fortschritts zu kreieren, die im Dienst des Lebens steht. Erfinden, um den Gedanken Konsistenz zu verleihen. Konstruieren, um dem Leben Substanz zu geben.

Massauds Leitidee ist, eine Symbiose zwischen „Kultur" und „Natur", zwischen „Technosphäre" und „Ökosphäre", zwischen dem Mensch und seiner Umgebung herzustellen. Er bemüht sich, das Verhältnis zwischen Mensch und Natur nicht nur durch spektakuläre Bauten, sondern auch in alltäglichen Gegenständen herauszuarbeiten. Durch die Beschäftigung mit städtebaulichen Aspekten entdeckte er die enge Verknüpfung zwischen Design und Architektur und deren Wirkung auf Mensch und Umwelt. „Architektur zu machen läuft darauf hinaus, Ökosysteme zu konzipieren".

Massaud setzt sich für einen alternativen Konsumumgang ein. Gemäß dem Motto „nicht mehr, sondern besser", möchte er unsere Lebens- und Erfahrungsqualität verbessern.

Marktwirtschaft basiert auf Wachstum. Quantitatives Wachstum muss dringend zu qualitativem Wachstum wechseln, weil die Erde ein endliches System ist.

Gegenstände sind nichts als Worte, die uns erlauben, Sätze zu schreiben, Geschichten zu verfassen, unsere Umgebung zu konstruieren. Sie müssen also Sinnes- und Gefühlträger sein.

In der für ihn richtungslosen Gesellschaft darf der Designer nicht länger die Funktion eines naiven oder zynischen Formgestalters haben, sondern die eines Szenaristen unserer Umwelt. Massaud betrachtet den Designer als gewissenhaften Katalysator der Ziele seiner Epoche, der alternative Modelle für verantwortlichen Konsum vorschlagen muss. Überzeugt davon, dass es für den Menschen unbedingt notwendig ist, sich neu zu erfinden, sein individuelles und kollektives Lebensprojekt wirklich zu definieren, sieht Jean-Marie Massaud sein Werk in einer engagierten und resoluten politischen Richtung. „Der Fortschritt wird menschlich sein oder er wird nie existieren."

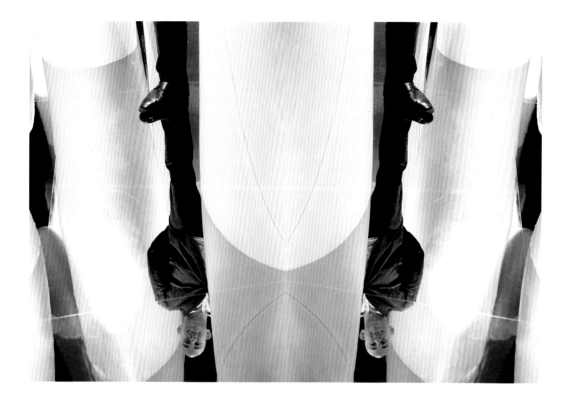

Design is nothing. Life is everything.

De niño Jean-Marie Massaud quería ser inventor. Este deseo se convirtió en realidad. Hoy en día no le interesa crear utopías sino una visión humana del progreso perdurable, que esté al servicio de la vida. Inventar para dar consistencia a la idea. Construir para dotar de sustancia a la vida.

La idea directriz de Massaud es realizar una simbiosis entre "cultura" y "naturaleza", entre "tecnoesfera" y "ecoesfera", entre ser humano y entorno. Procura realizar la relación entre ser humano y naturaleza y no sólo con espectaculares edificios, sino también en los objetos cotidianos. Al ocuparse de cuestiones urbanísticas descubrió la estrecha conexión entre diseño y arquitectura, así como su efecto sobre el ser humano y el medioambiente. "Crear arquitectura desemboca en concebir ecosistemas".

Massaud está a favor de mantener una relación alternativa con el consumo. De acuerdo con el lema "no más, sino mejor", quiere mejorar nuestra calidad de vida y experiencia.

La economía de mercado se basa en el crecimiento. El crecimiento cuantitativo ha de mutar urgentemente en crecimiento cualitativo, porque la Tierra es un sistema finito.

Los objetos no son más que palabras que nos permiten escribir frases, relatar historias, construir nuestro entorno. Tienen que ser portadores de sentido y sensibilidad.

En la sociedad, que en su opinión carece de rumbo, el diseñador ya no puede seguir siendo un estilista ingenuo o cínico, sino un escenógrafo de nuestro medioambiente. Massaud contempla al diseñador como a un concienzudo catalizador de los objetivos de nuestra época, que debe proponer modelos alternativos para un consumo responsable. Convencido de que el ser humano necesita urgentemente inventarse de nuevo y definir verdaderamente su proyecto vital tanto a nivel individual, como colectivo, Jean-Marie Massaud contempla su obra de un modo comprometido y decididamente político. "El progreso será humano o no será nada."

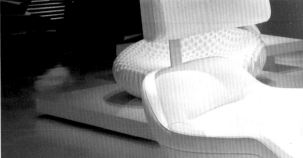

Design is nothing. Life is everything.

Comme enfant, Jean-Marie Massaud voulait devenir inventeur. Il réalisait ce désir. Aujourd'hui, il ne s'agit pas pour lui de créer des utopies, mais une vision humaine du progrès qui est au service de la vie dans son ensemble. Inventer pour céder de la concistance aux pensées. Construire pour donner de la substance à la vie.

Le leitmotiv de Massaud est de créer une symbiose entre « Culture » et « Nature », entre « technosphère » et « écosphère », entre l'homme et son environnement. Il s'efforce de faire ressortir le rapport entre l'homme et la nature non seulement par des bâtiments spectaculaires, mais aussi par des objets quotidiens. Par l'occupation avec des questions d'urbanisme, il découvrait la liaison étroite entre le design et l'architecture et ses effets sur la vie de l'homme et de son environnement. « Faire de l'architecture revient à concevoir des écosystèmes ».

Massaud favorise un rapport alternatif avec la consommation. Selon la devise « il faut passer de l'économie du plus à l'économie du mieux », il veut améliorer notre qualité et expérience de la vie.

L'économie de marché est basée sur la croissance. Il est urgent de muter de la croissance quantitative à la croissance qualitative, car la terre est un système fini.

Les objets ne sont que des mots qui nous permettent d'écrire des phrases, de composer des histoires, de construire notre environnement. Ils doivent donc être porteur de sens et d'émotion.

Dans une société selon lui sans repères, la fonction du designer ne peut plus être celle d'un styliste naïf ou cynique, mais celle d'un scénariste de notre environnement. Massaud considère le designer comme catalyseur conscient des enjeux de son époque, qui doit proposer de models alternatifs de consommation responsable. Puisqu'il est convaincu qu'il est absolument nécessaire pour l'homme de se réinventer, de réellement définir son projet de vie, individuel et collectif, Jean-Marie Massaud voit son œuvre dans un chemin politique résolu et engagé.

« Le progrès sera humain ou ne sera plus ».

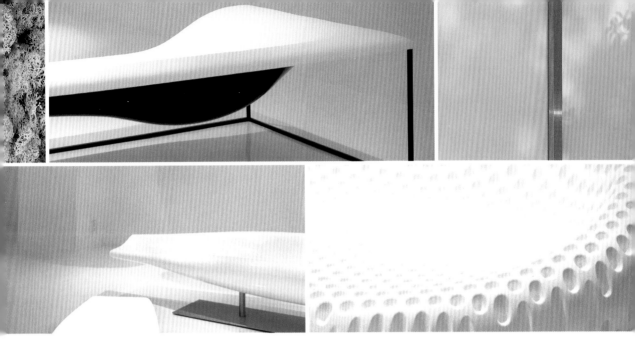

Design is nothing. Life is everything.

Nella sua infanzia Jean-Marie Massaud sognava di divenire inventore. Tale desiderio si avverò. Oggi non gli interessa creare utopie, ma realizzare una visione umana del progresso sostenibile, che sia al servizio della vita. Inventare per dare consistenza ai pensieri. Costruire per dare sostanza alla vita.

L'idea guida di Massaud è generare una simbiosi tra "cultura" e "natura", "tecnosfera" ed "ecosfera", tra l'uomo e l'ambiente. Si impegna ad ottenere il rapporto tra essere umano e natura non soltanto attraverso costruzioni spetta-colari ma anche tramite oggetti del quotidiano. Essendosi dedicato ai temi urbanistici, scoprì lo stretto legame tra design e architettura e la loro influenza sugli uomini e l'ambiente. "Fare architettura equivale a concepire degli eco-sistemi".

Massaud favorisce un rapporto alternativo nei confronti del consumo. Secondo il motto "transitare dall'economia del più all'economia del meglio", ambisce a migliorare la nostra qualità ed esperienza della vita.

L'economia di mercato è basata sulla crescita. La crescita quantitativa deve mutare urgentemente in crescita quali-tativa, dal momento che la terra è un sistema finito.

Gli oggetti non sono altro che parole che ci permettono di scrivere frasi, di comporre delle storie, di costruire il nostro ambiente. Devono dunque essere portatori di senso e di emozioni.

Nella società, a suo avviso senza direzione, la funzione del designer non può più rimanere quella di uno stilista ingenuo o cinico, ma piuttosto quella di uno scenografo del nostro ambiente. Massaud considera il designer come catalizzatore coscienzioso delle mete della sua epoca che ha il compito di proporre modelli alternativi in merito al consumo respon-sabile. Convinto che sia urgentemente necessario per l'uomo di reinventarsi, di definire realmente il proprio progetto esistenziale individuale e collettivo, Jean-Marie Massaud ritiene la sua opera una direzione politica risoluta. "Il pro-gresso o sarà umano o non ci sarà."

ARCHITECTURE

All the following architectural projects are the fruits of the collaboration of Jean-Marie Massaud and Daniel Pouzet.

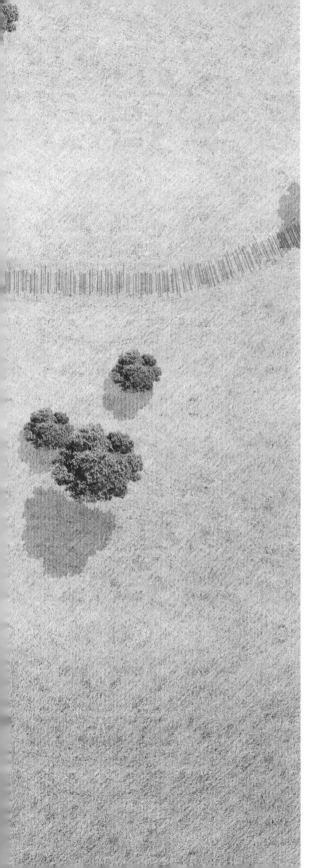

TANABE HOUSE
PRIVATE RESIDENCE | FUKUOKA, JAPAN, 1999
Client: Private
Surface area: 450 m^2

Vital and cultural background – The Tanabe house is a shelter inspired from unexpressed desires, specific to the Japanese context. It is build according to the cultural and instinctive need for protection and well being. The house disappears from the street to appear like a burrow. A strip of land houses a large interior open plan. Unsuspected from the street, it is widely opened onto the garden. A frontier-like bookcase organizes the space. Cabin-like bedrooms hang from the roof garden. The roof garden extends and reveals the vital and intimate territory of the family living inside.

Vitaler und kultureller Hintergrund – Als Rückzugsort inspiriert sich das Haus Tanabe an, für den japanischen Kontext spezifischen, unausgedrückten Wünschen und antwortet auf die kulturelle und instinktive Notwendigkeit nach Schutz und Wohlbefinden. Wie ein Kaninchenbau ist das Haus von der Strasse aus unsichtbar. Ein grüner Schutzmantel birgt einen großzügigen offenen Grundriss unter sich, der sich zum Garten weit öffnet. Eine große Bücherwand unterteilt den Raum. Die Schlafzimmer wirken wie Kabinen und hängen vom Dachgarten herab, welcher das lebendige und intime Territorium der Familie ausdehnt und zum Vorschein bringt.

Trasfondo vital y cultural – La casa Tanabe es un refugio inspirado por deseos inexpresados, específicos del contexto japonés. Está construida de acuerdo con la necesidad cultural e instintiva de protección y bienestar. La casa desaparece de la calle y se muestra como una madriguera. Una franja de terreno alberga un gran plano interior abierto. Pasa desapercibida desde la calle y se abre ampliamente sobre el jardín. Una librería similar a una frontera organiza el espacio. Dormitorios que se asemejan a camarotes cuelgan de la azotea. La azotea extiende y revela el territorio vital e íntimo de la familia que vive en el interior.

Enjeux ressentis vitaux et acquis culturels – La maison Tanabé est un refuge, un abri, qui est imaginé à partir de désirs non exprimés, propres au contexte japonais. Elle repose sur la nécessité culturelle et instinctive de bien-être et de protection. Depuis la rue, la maison disparaît et apparaît comme un terrier. Une langue de terre abrite un grand plan libre intérieur insoupçonnable protégé de la rue et généreusement ouvert côté jardin. Une bibliothèque-frontière articule l'espace. Les chambres-cabanes sont suspendues au jardin-toiture. Ce toit-jardin prolonge et révèle le territoire vital et intime de la famille qu'il abrite.

Sfondo vitale e culturale – Come un rifugio ispirato da desideri inespressi – specifici per il contesto giapponese – la casa Tanabe risponde alla necessità culturale e istintiva del benessere e della protezione. La casa interrata assomiglia quasi ad una tana. Invisibile dalla strada, si apre verso il giardino. Un manto verde copre una pianta libera all'interno, il cui spazio viene articolato da una libreria che funge da frontiera. Le camere sembrano cabine sospese dal giardino pensile che estende e rivela il territorio vitale ed intimo della famiglia che lì vive.

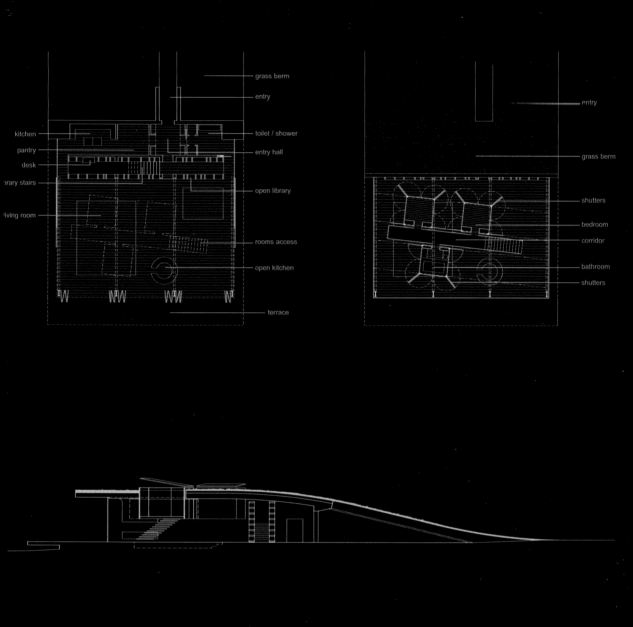

grass berm

entry

kitchen

pantry

desk

library stairs

living room

toilet / shower

entry hall

open library

rooms access

open kitchen

terrace

entry

grass berm

shutters

bedroom

corridor

bathroom

shutters

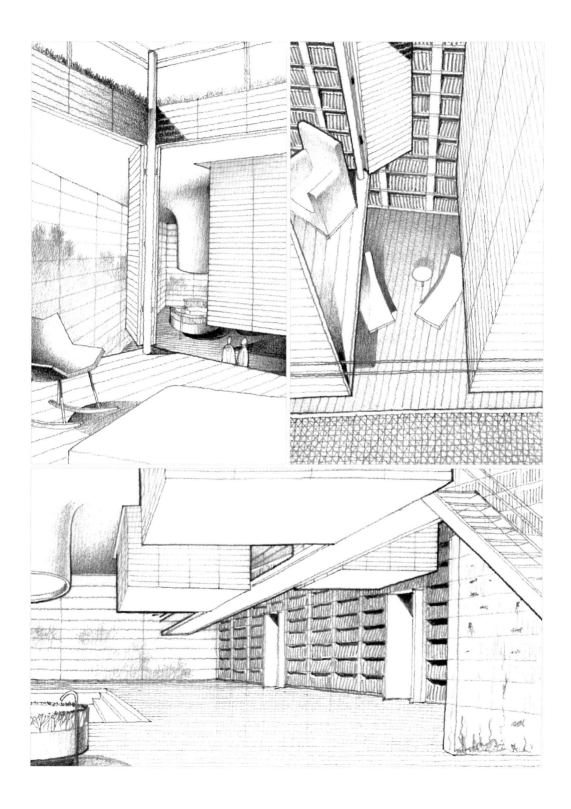

HOTEL MAHN
SPA HOTEL / PROJECT | PUERTO VALLARTA, MEXICO, 2003
Client: Omnilife
Surface area: 15.000 m^2

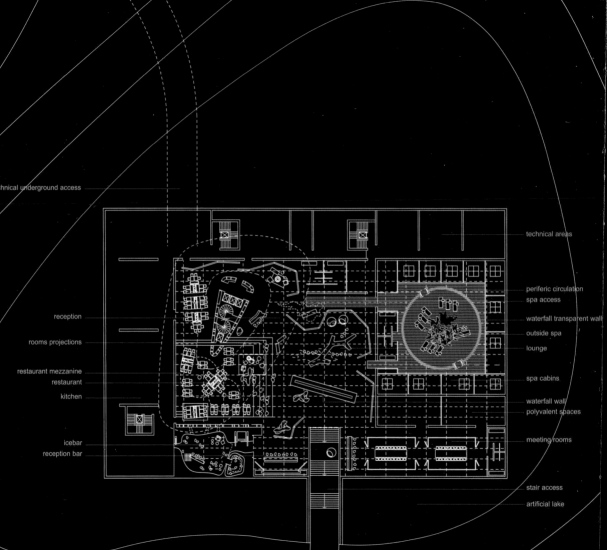

technical underground access

technical areas

periferic circulation
spa access

reception

waterfall transparent wall

rooms projections

outside spa

lounge

restaurant mezzanine
restaurant

spa cabins

kitchen

waterfall wall
polyvalent spaces

icebar
reception bar

meeting rooms

stair access

artificial lake

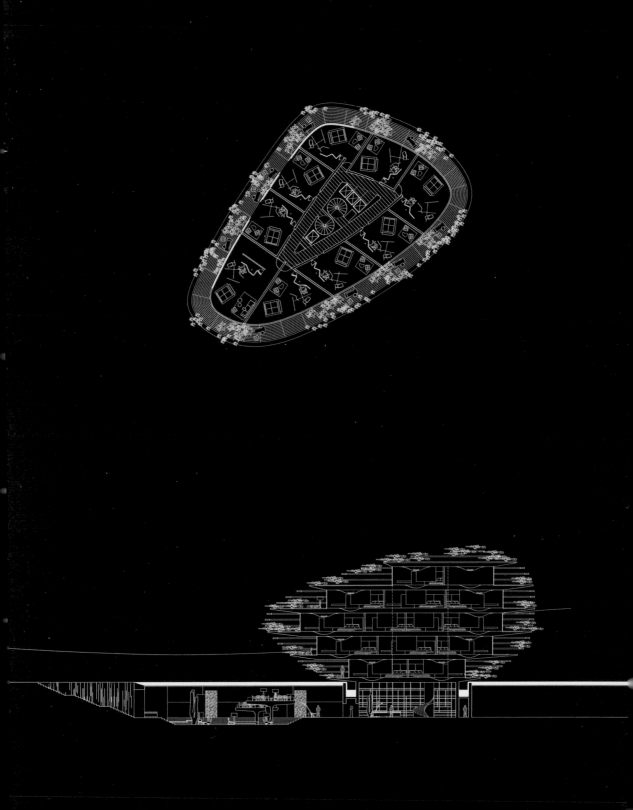

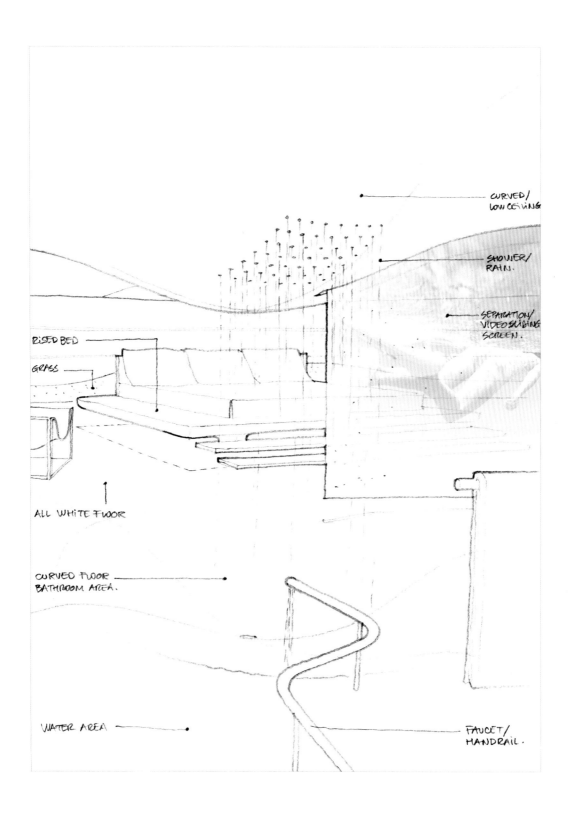

CURVED/
LOW CEILING

SHOWER/
RAIN.

SEPARATION/
VIDEO SLIDING
SCREEN.

RISED BED

GRASS

ALL WHITE FLOOR

CURVED FLOOR
BATHROOM AREA.

WATER AREA

FAUCET/
HANDRAIL.

Serenity – Visitors are submerged in a deconcerting universe: a physical and emotional well-being's sanctuary. As a recurrent component, water is treated like an energy materializing itself in adequacy with the intended atmosphere. The hotel – like a pebble invaded by plants – stands on a quiet lake which covers the public spaces. The access is a biblical one: visitors walk on water and go through a liquid curtain poring along colossal stairs. The spa remains concealed under a still water mirror. Based in the pebble, bedrooms are protected from the world by the lake.

Heiterkeit – Der Besucher taucht in ein Universum ein, in dem er sämtliche Bezugspunkte verliert, in ein Heiligtum physischen und emotionalen Wohlbefindens. Das häufig vorkommende Element Wasser wird wie Energie behandelt, die sich in Funktion der beabsichtigten Atmosphäre gestaltet. Das Hotel gleicht einem von Pflanzen kolonisierten Kiesel, liegt auf einer stillen Wasserfläche und bedeckt die öffentlichen Bereiche. Der Zugang vollzieht sich auf biblische Art: Man geht auf Wasser und wandelt durch einen flüssigen Vorhang, der eine mächtige Treppe entlang fliesst. Der Spa-Bereich befindet sich unter dem ruhigen Wasserspiegel. Die Zimmer im Inneren des Kiesels sind durch den See vor der Welt geschützt.

Serenidad – Los visitantes se sumergen en un universo desconcertante: un santuario de bienestar físico y emocional. Como un componente recurrente, el agua es tratada como energía que se materializa a sí misma en consonancia con la atmósfera deseada. El hotel – como un guijarro invadido por la vegetación – se levanta sobre un lago tranquilo que cubre los espacios públicos. El acceso es bíblico: los visitantes caminan sobre el agua y atraviesan una cortina líquida que fluye a lo largo de colosales escalones. El spa permanece escondido bajo un inmóvil espejo de agua. Afianzados en el guijarro, el lago protege a los dormitorios frente al mundo.

Sérénité – Le visiteur s'immerge dans un univers où il perd tous ses repères, un sanctuaire du bien être physique et émotionnel. L'eau, élément récurrent, y est traitée comme une énergie, se matérialisant en fonction de l'atmosphère recherchée. L'hôtel, galet colonisé par le végétal, est posé sur une nappe d'eau calme recouvrant les parties publiques. On y accède bibliquement, en marchant sur l'eau puis en traversant un rideau liquide s'écoulant le long d'un escalier magistral. Le Spa est dissimulé sous un miroir d'eau calme. Les chambres, situées dans le galet, sont protégées du monde grâce au lac.

Serenità – Il visitatore s'immerge in un universo dove perde tutti i suoi riferimenti, un santuario di benessere fisico ed emotivo. L'acqua, elemento ricorrente, viene trattata come un'energia che si materializza in funzione dell'atmosfera ricercata. L'albergo, ciottolo colonizzato da piante, giace su una superficie d'acqua che ricopre le parti pubbliche. L'accesso si sviluppa secondo modalità quasi bibliche: camminando sull'acqua, si attraversa una tenda liquida che scorre lungo imponenti scale. La zona spa si trova sotto il calmo specchio d'acqua. Le camere situate all'interno del ciottolo sono protette dal mondo esterno tramite il lago.

CURTAIN

TRANPARENCE
TGHROW WATE

PASSAGE TO
SPA

TEACK DECK

23

MAMA SHELTER RESORT HOTEL
PALM DESERT | CALIFORNIA, USA, 2003
Client: Town & Shelter
Surface area: 28.700 m^2
250 bungalows + 8 artist residences

The architecture with its structure, style and outer shell reveals the profound nature of the place; akin to a reef of life that enables all sorts of encounters and encourages all kinds of influences. Enshrouded by a screen of plants, the original singular monolithic space is delineated, thus creating vital room for respiration and a certain tangibility at the same time. The flux of light and people permeates the very heart of the building. Openings reveal creative idiosyncracies; the vertebral articulations of the hotel.

Die Struktur, die Ausführung und die Hülle der Architektur kristallisieren die tiefe Natur des Ortes, ein Lebensriff, das jegliche Art von Begegnungen und Einflüssen ermöglicht. Von einem Sieb aus Pflanzen umgeben, ist der monolithische Körper in Teilen ausgeschnitten, um lebensnotwendiges Atmen und Versorgung bereitzustellen. Der Licht- und Öffentlichkeitsfluss dringen bis zum Herzen des Gebäudes durch. Öffnungen lassen fruchtbare Eigenheiten, die Gliederung des Hotels, in Erscheinung treten.

En su estructura, sus articulaciones y su envoltura, la arquitectura cristaliza la naturaleza profunda del lugar; un arrecife de agua donde son posibles todos los reencuentros e influencias. Aureolado por un tamiz vegetal, el volumen monolítico natural se ensancha para crear respiración e innervación vitales. El flujo de la luz y del público penetran hasta el corazón mismo del edificio. Surgen orificios de singularidades fecundas, las articulaciones vertebrales del hotel.

L'architecture dans sa structure, ses articulations et son enveloppe, cristallise la nature profonde du lieu; un récif de vie où toutes rencontres et influences sont possibles. Nimbé d'un tamis végétal, le volume monolithique natif est échancré pour créer respiration et innervation vitales. Le flux de la lumière et du public pénétrant jusqu'au cœur même de l'édifice. Des percées surgissent de fécondes singularités, les articulations vertébrales de l'hôtel.

L'architettura nella sua struttura, nelle sue articolazioni e nel suo involucro cristallizza la natura profonda del luogo; una barriera di vita dove sono possibili tutti gli incontri e tutti gli influssi. Avvolto da un filtro vegetale, il volume monolitico originario è scavato per creare una respirazione e un'innervazione vitale; il flusso della luce e del pubblico penetra nel cuore dell'edificio, e le aperture nascono da feconde individualità, le articolazioni vertebrali dell'hotel.

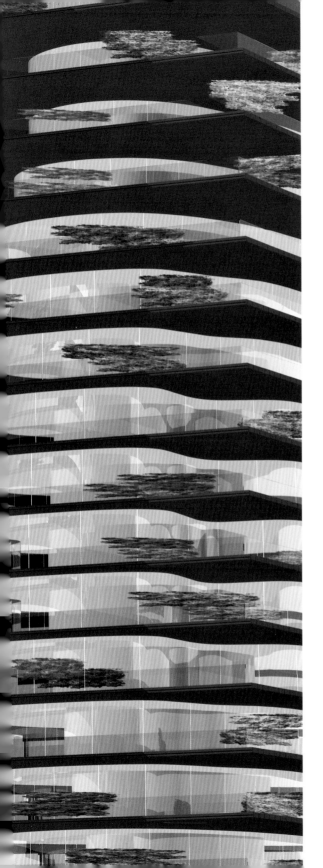

LIFE REEF
HOUSING HIGH-RISE |
GUADALAJARA, MEXICO, 2003
Client: Omnilife
Surface area: 12.000 m²
102 condominium units
Opening: March 2007

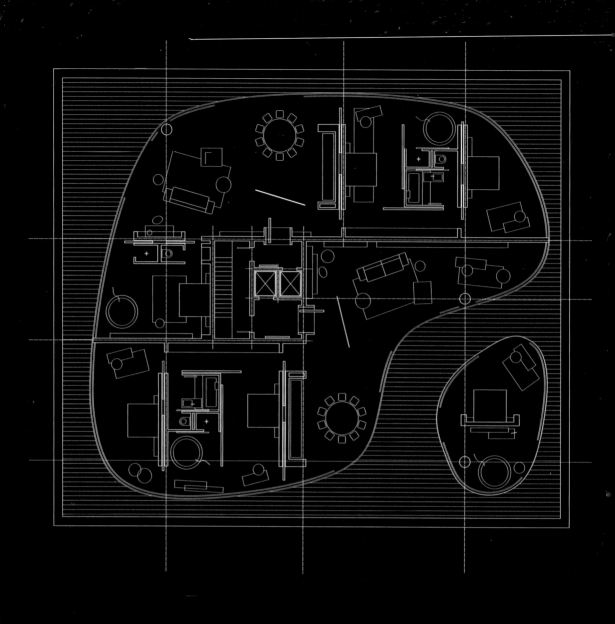

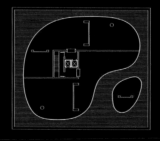
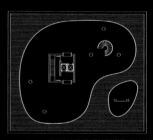

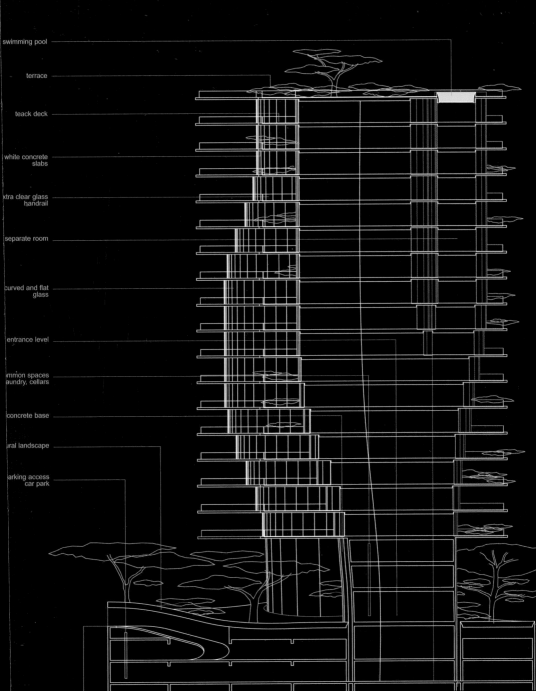

swimming pool

terrace

teack deck

white concrete
slabs

xtra clear glass
handrail

separate room

curved and flat
glass

entrance level

mmon spaces
aundry, cellars

concrete base

ural landscape

arking access
car park

Life Reef is not a "housing machine" but a lively space. These towers are superpositions of private lands, affording unique views. Building vertically in a urban environment which tends to develop itself horizontally, usually induces the raising of a strong but authoritarian sign. Life Reef is supposed to be a different option. Sensual growing outlines are protected by a virtual volume which is defined by terraces. Each floor opens up to the horizon but preserves its intimacy. Each flat and its terrace creates a feeling of appropriation and a fertile settlement. Colonized by vegetation, the high-rises generate their own diversity.

Life Reef ist keine „Wohnmaschine", sondern ein lebendiger Ort. Die Türme stellen eine senkrechte Anordnung privaten Grunds dar und bieten einzigartige Ausblicke. Vertikal in einer urbanen Umgebung zu bauen, welche dazu tendiert, sich horizontal auszudehnen, führt normalerweise das Aufkommen eines starken autoritären Zeichens herbei. Life Reef will eine andere Option bieten. Ein virtuelles, durch Terrassen definiertes Volumen, schützt sinnliche Silhouetten. Jedes Geschoss öffnet sich zum Horizont, behält jedoch seine Privatheit bei. Jede Wohnung mit samt Terrasse erzeugt ein Gefühl von Aneignung und von fruchtbarer Ansiedlung. Der Pflanzenbewuchs gibt den Hochhäusern ihren besonderen Charakter.

Life Reef no es una "máquina donde vivir" sino un espacio vivo. Estas torres son superposiciones de terrenos privados que ofrecen unas vistas únicas. Construir verticalmente en un entorno urbano, que de por sí tiende a desarrollarse horizontalmente, suele inducir a la eclosión de un signo fuerte pero autoritario. Life Reef intenta ser una opción diferente. Los contornos, que crecen sensualmente, están protegidos por un volumen virtual definido por terrazas. Cada uno de los pisos se abre al horizonte pero preserva a la vez su intimidad. Cada una de las viviendas con su terraza crea un sentimiento de apropiación y de asentamiento fértil. Colonizados por la vegetación los rascacielos generan su propia diversidad.

Life Reef n'est pas une « machine à habiter » mais un lieu vivant. Ces tours sont des superpositions de terrains personnels qui proposent des horizons uniques. Construire à la verticale dans un espace urbain qui tend à se développer à l'horizontal induit généralement l'érection d'un signe fort mais autoritaire. Life Reef se veut une autre voie. Des silhouettes sensuelles sont protégées par un volume virtuel défini par des terrasses. Chaque étage s'ouvre sur l'horizon, mais préserve son intimité. Chaque appartement et sa terrasse créent un sentiment d'appropriation et de colonisation fertile. Colonisées par la végétation, elles créent leur propre diversité.

Life Reef non è una "macchina per abitare" ma un luogo vivo. Le torri rappresentano sovrapposizioni di terreno privato che offrono una vista unica. Costruire in verticale in un contesto urbano che di per sé tende a svilupparsi in modo orizzontale, induce generalmente la nascita di un segno forte e autoritario. Life Reef vuol dare un'opzione differente. Un volume virtuale definito da terrazze protegge sagome sensuali. Tutti i piani si aprono verso l'orizzonte, pur preservando la loro intimità. Ogni appartamento terrazzato crea una sensazione di appropriazione e di insediamento fertile. La colonizzazione vegetale conferisce alle le torri un carattere speciale.

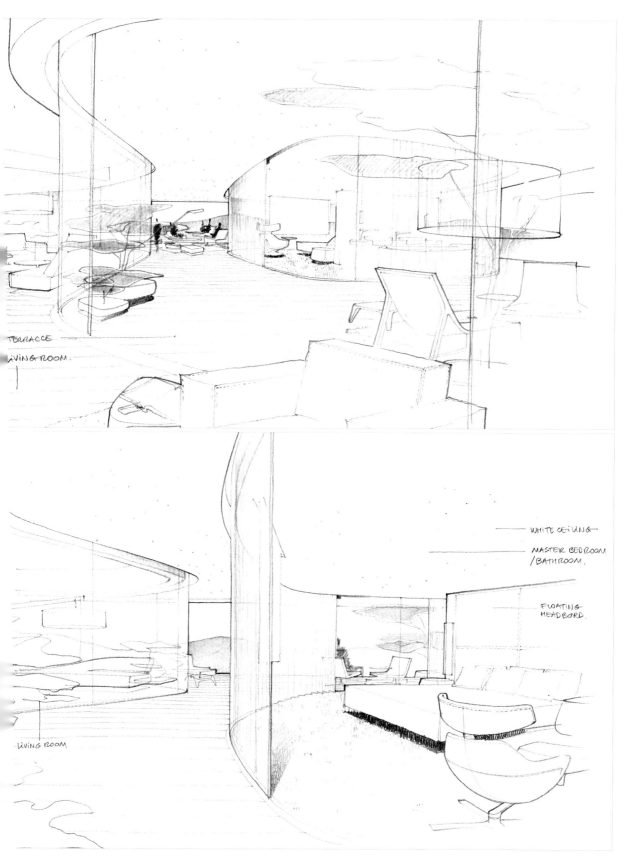

TERRACCE

LIVING ROOM.

WHITE CEILING

MASTER BEDROOM
/BATHROOM.

FLOATING
HEADBORD

LIVING ROOM

VOLCANO STADIUM

FOOTBALL STADIUM | GUADALAJARA, MEXICO, 2003-2007
Client: Omnilife
Surface area: 110.000 m²
Capacity: 45.000 places
Technical architecture: HOK + SVE
Structure: Luis Bozzo Estructuras SL

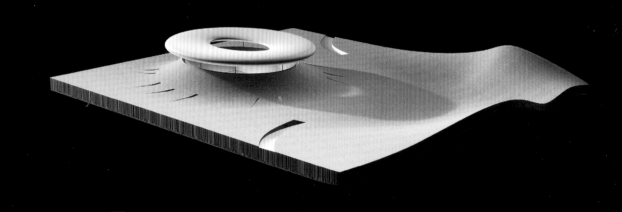

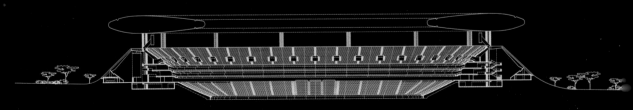

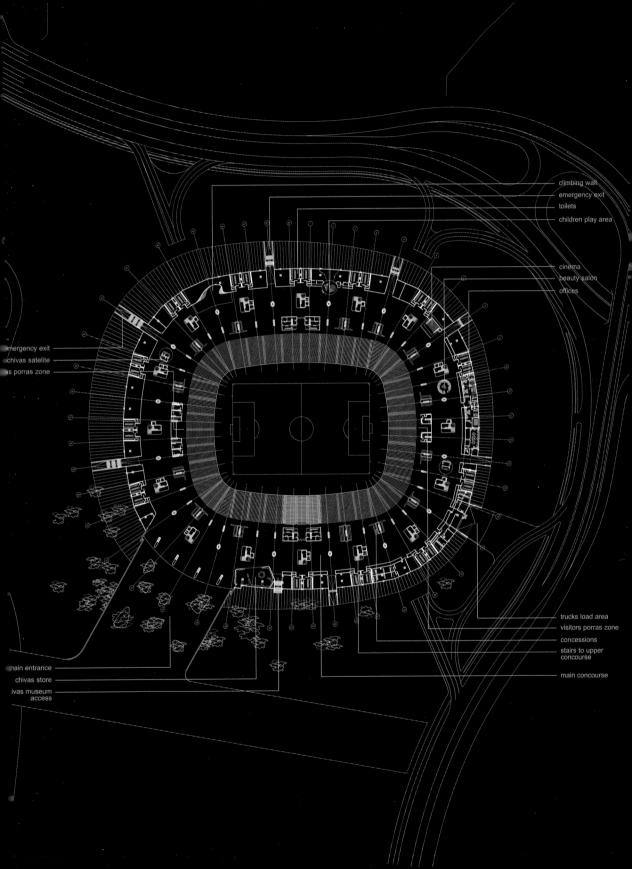

climbing wall
emergency exit
toilets
children play area

cinema
beauty salon
offices

emergency exit
chivas satelite
as porras zone

trucks load area
visitors porras zone
concessions
stairs to upper
concourse

main concourse

main entrance
chivas store
ivas museum
access

Create a harmony with either an absence of energy or an excess of energy

Stadiums are places of popular sharing. Beyond scale, they create urban no man's lands, becoming ideal stages for hooligans. Volcano Stadium is first of all a lively place built around man and his environment. Expanding the landscape, the architecture expresses a symbol of life: an ecosystem favouring a peaceful local life while hosting major cultural or sports events. The architecture reflects its underlying symbols. The volcano represents the telluric energy while the semi-floating cloud conveys this energy to the city. The place becomes part of the community identity, where one can take a walk and enjoy unique views on the city of Guadalajara.

Harmonie mit entweder zu viel oder zu wenig Energie erzeugen

Stadien sind Orte allgemeinen Zusammenkommens. Jenseits jeglichen Maßstabs erzeugen sie städtische no man's lands und sind ideale Treffpunkte für hooligans. Volcano Stadium ist vor allem ein lebendiger Ort, um den Menschen und seine Umgebung herum gebaut. Als Landschaftserweiterung behauptet sich die Architektur als ein Lebenssymbol: ein Ökosystem, das ein friedvolles örtliches Leben begünstigt und gleichzeitig bedeutende kulturelle oder sportliche Veranstaltungen beherbergt. Der Bau bildet seine ihm zugrunde liegenden Symbole ab. Der Vulkan stellt die tellurische Energie dar, während die schwebende Wolke diese zur Stadt leitet. Der Ort bildet die Identität der Gemeinschaft und lädt zum spazieren gehen und zum genießen einzigartiger Ausblicke auf die Stadt Guadalajara ein.

Crear una armonía sin ausencia o exceso de energía

Los estadios son lugares de participación popular. Si superan la medida, crean tierras urbanas de nadie que se convierten en escenarios ideales para hooligans. El Volcano Stadium es, ante todo, un lugar vivo construido en torno al hombre y su entorno. Expandiendo el paisaje, la arquitectura expresa un símbolo de vida: un ecosistema que favorece una pacífica vida local a la vez que alberga grandes acontecimientos culturales y deportivos. La arquitectura refleja sus símbolos subyacentes. El volcán representa la energía telúrica, mientras que la nube semiflotante dirige esta energía hacia la ciudad. El lugar se convierte en parte de la identidad comunitaria, un sitio donde se puede dar un paseo y disfrutar de las incomparables vistas de la ciudad de Guadalajara.

Harmoniser un trop plein ou une absence d'énergie

Les stades sont des lieux de communion populaire. Hors de toute échelle, ils créent des no man's lands urbains, scènes rêvées pour les hooligans. Volcano Stadium est d'abord un lieu vivant construit autour de l'homme et de son environnement. Extension du paysage, l'architecture s'affirme en symbole de vie: un écosystême propice ê l'épanouissement d'une vie locale paisible et ê l'accueil d'événements sportifs ou culturels débordants. L'architecture est ê l'image de ses symboles fondateurs. Le volcan représente l'énergie tellurique, le nuage semi-flottant révèle cette énergie ê la ville. Cette architecture devient un élément identitaire de la communauté, un lieu de promenade et un point d'observation privilégié de la ville de Guadalajara.

Creare armonia con assenza o con eccesso d'energia

Gli stadi sono luoghi di comunione popolare. Fuori scala creano terre di nessuno nel tessuto urbano, palcoscenico ideale per hooligans. Volcano Stadium è anzitutto un luogo vivo, costruito intorno all'essere umano e al suo ambiente. L'architettura, estensione del paesaggio, è un simbolo di vita: un ecosistema propizio ad una vita locale pacifica e in grado di accogliere eventi sportivi o culturali. La costruzione riflette i suoi simboli fondatori. Il vulcano simbolizza un'energia tellurica, mentre la nuvola sospesa trasmette quest'energia alla città. L'architettura diventa così un elemento identitario della comunità, un luogo di passeggiate con scorci particolari sulla città di Guadalajara.

TRIB'TRIBE HUT
CONDOMINIUM TOWER / TRIBECA |
NEW YORK, USA, 2004
Surface area: 35.000 m^2
24 lofts, 6 townhouses, 125 condominiums
with shops
Opening: November 2008

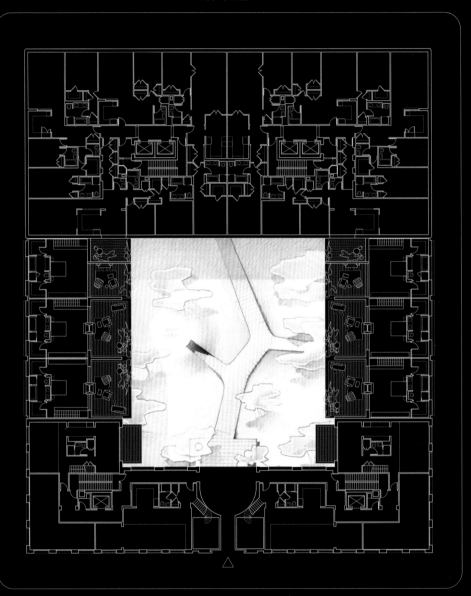

WEST STREET

DEBROSSES STREET

WATTS STREET

WASHINGTON STREET

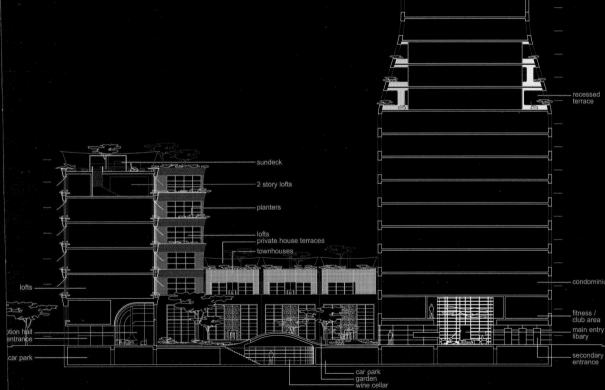

sundeck

2 story lofts

planters

lofts
private house terraces

townhouses

lofts

recessed
terrace

condominiu

fitness /
club area

main entry
libary

secondary
entrance

ption hall
entrance

car park

car park
garden
wine cellar

DEAN & DELUCA

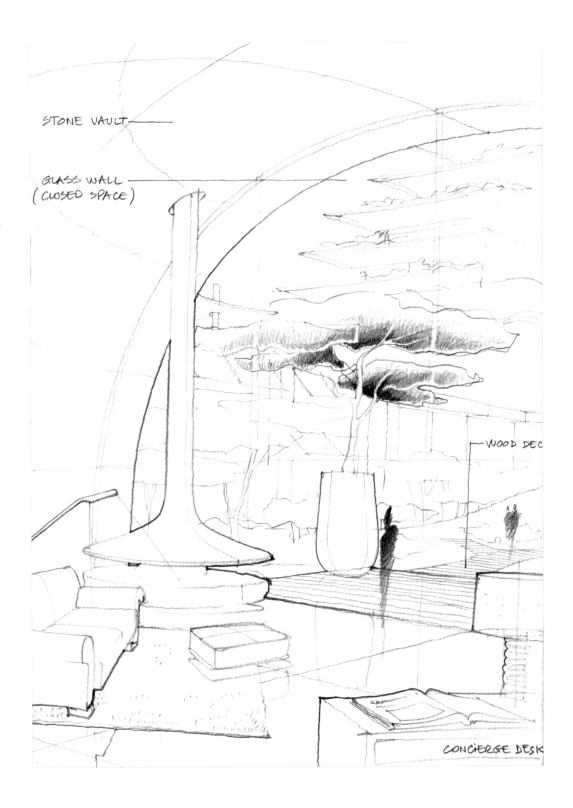

STONE VAULT ————

GLASS WALL ————
(CLOSED SPACE)

WOOD DEC

CONCIERGE DESK

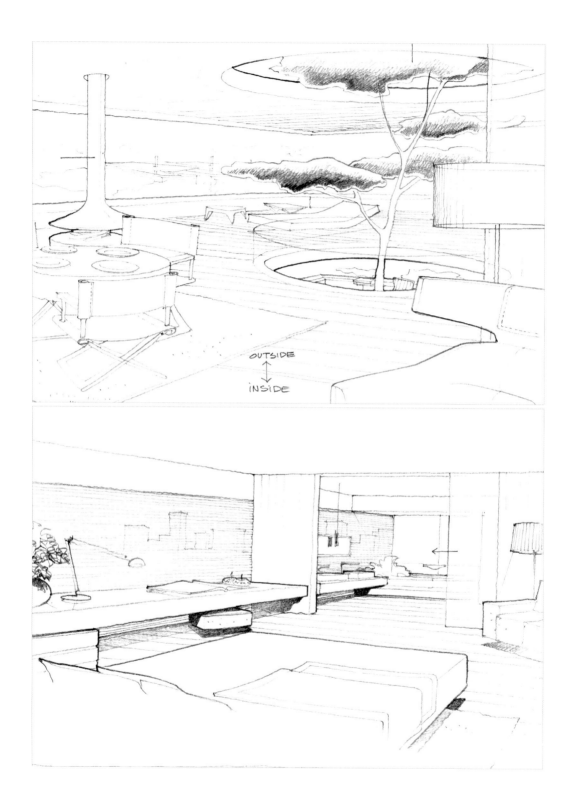

OUTSIDE
↑
↓
INSIDE

NANTUCKET HOUSE
PRIVATE RESIDENCE | NANTUCKET, USA, 2005
Client: Privat
Surface area: 1.500 m²
Technical architecture: Andrew Kochen

SWIMING POOL

1ST LEVEL
ADAM'S OFFICE
2ND LEVEL
MASTER BEDROOM.

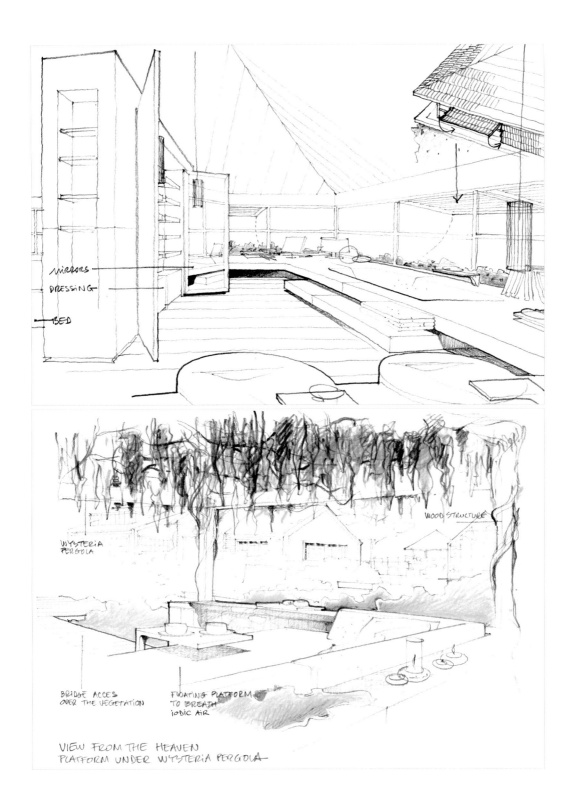

MIRRORS
DRESSING
BED

WYSTERIA
PERGOLA

WOOD STRUCTURE

BRIDGE ACCES
OVER THE VEGETATION

FLOATING PLATFORM
TO BREATH
IODIC AIR

VIEW FROM THE HEAVEN
PLATFORM UNDER WYSTERIA PERGOLA

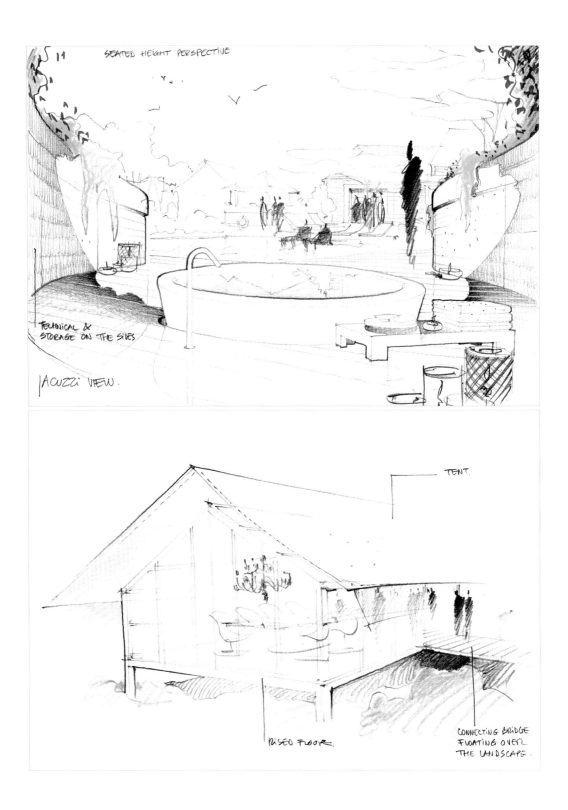

SEATED HEIGHT PERSPECTIVE

TECHNICAL &
STORAGE ON THE SIDES

JACUZZI VIEW.

TENT.

RAISED FLOOR.

CONNECTING BRIDGE
FLOATING OVER
THE LANDSCAPE.

SWIMMING POOL

VIEW FROM THE OUTSIDE SOFA.

INTERIOR

All the following interior projects are the fruits of the collaboration of Jean-Marie Massaud and Daniel Pouzet.

SEPHORA BLANC
CONCEPT FOR SALES OUTLET | PARIS, 2000
Client: Sephora, France
Surface area: 300 m^2

A place to initiate people to interior harmony. From rough materials to sophisticated and then sublimated ones (energy, culture...), this space presents well-being, care and its ritual through different cultures in a continuous evolution. It is a space invaded by a light which defines and puts a sparkle in volumes. It is simply the proof that energy is more important than materials.

Ein Ort, der Anstoß zur inneren Harmonie gibt. Von groben zu „kultivierten" und sublimierten Materialien (Energie, Kultur,...), zeigt der Ort in kontinuierlicher Evolution Wohlbefinden, Pflege und ihre Ritualien anhand verschiedener Kulturen. Ort des Erwachens von Licht durchflutet, das seine Volumina definiert und animiert. Der Beweis dafür, dass Energie wichtiger als Material ist.

Un lugar para iniciar a la gente en la energía interior. Desde los materiales toscos a los sofisticados y luego a los sublimados, (energía, cultura...), este espacio presenta el bienestar, el cuidado y su ritual a través de culturas diferentes en una evolución continua. Se trata de un espacio invadido por una luz que define y aporta brillo a los volúmenes. Es la prueba absoluta de que la energía es más importante que los materiales.

Lieu d'initiation à l'harmonie intérieure. De la matière brute, à la matière raffinée, puis sublimée (énergie, culture...), cet espace présente le bien-être, le soin et ses rites au travers de différentes cultures dans une perpétuelle évolution. Lieu d'éveil habité par la lumière qui anime et en définit les volumes. Preuve que l'énergie est plus importante que la matière.

Luogo d'iniziazione all'armonia interiore. Da materiali grezzi a materiali raffinati, poi sublimati (energia, cultura,...), questo luogo presenta il benessere, la cura e i suoi rituali attraverso culture differenti in continua evoluzione. Luogo di risveglio, invaso dalla luce che definisce e anima i volumi. Prova che l'energia è più importante della materia.

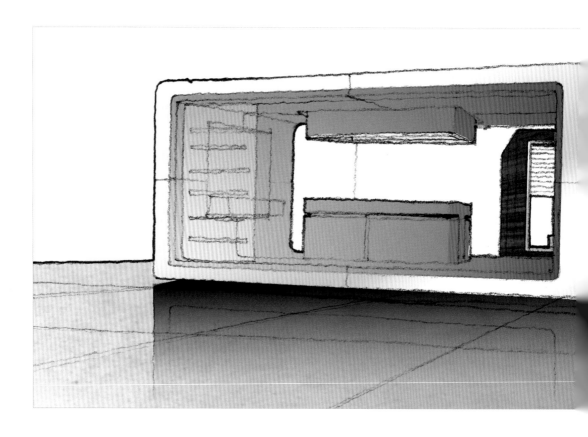

LOFT UNITS
LIVING IN FURNITURE | CONCEPT, 2001
Dimensions: 2.200 x 3.500 x 2.500 mm

To overpass the traditional plans' sharing where partitions define each room following a central activity, Loft Units suggests inhabiting furniture's islands, like rocks on which life takes birth. Hidden, when you wish, they describe an environment open to plenty of possible adjustments.

Dream Unit: relaxation and intellect, bedroom, dressing and fitted video (material: leather and wood)
Pure Unit: relaxation et feeling, body care (material: Corian© and lava)
Flavour Unit: relaxation and affect, a dream place fitting an aromatic garden (material: Corian© and stainless steel)

Um die traditionelle Raumgliederung zu überholen, in der Wände die Räume nach Aktivitäten definieren, schlägt Loft Units kleine Inseln, Wohnmöbel vor, wie Felsen, auf denen das Leben entsteht. Bei Bedarf versteckt, beschreiben sie eine grenzenlose Landschaft.

Dream Unit: Entspannung und Intellekt, Schlafzimmer, Umkleide und Video (Material: Leder und Holz)
Pure Unit: Entspannung und Gefühl, Körperpflege (Material: Corian© und Lava)
Flavour Unit: Entspannung und Affekt, ein Ort der Sinne mit Aromagarten (Material: Corian© und Edelstahl)

Para rebasar la división tradicional del plano, en la que las particiones definen cada habitación según una actividad central, Loft Units sugiere islas de mobiliario habitacionales como rocas en las que nace la vida. Cuando están ocultas, si así lo desea, describen un entorno abierto lleno de posibles modificaciones.

Dream Unit: relajación e intelecto; dormitorio, vestidor y video empotrado (material: cuero y madera)
Pure Unit: relajación y sensación; cuidado corporal (material: Corian© y lava)
Flavour Unit: relajación y afecto, un lugar de ensueño adaptado en un jardín aromático (material: Corian© y acero inoxidable)

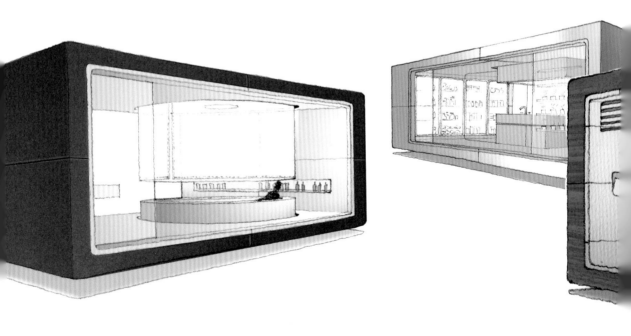

Pour dépasser la traditionnelle partition des plans dont les cloisons définissent les pièces par activité, Loft Units est une proposition d'îlots, de mobiliers habitables comme des récifs sur lesquels vient se greffer la vie. Occultables à souhait, ils décrivent un paysage aux perspectives ouvertes.

Dream Unit: détente et intellect, chambre, dressing et vidéo intégrée (materiaux: cuir et bois)
Pure Unit: détente et sensation, soins du corps (materiaux: Corian© et lave)
Flavour Unit: détente et affect, lieu du goût, intégrant un jardin aromatique (materiaux: Corian© et acier inoxydable)

Per superare la partizione tradizionale delle piante dove le pareti definiscono i vani per attività, Loft Units propone delle piccole isole, mobili abitabili come rocce sulle quali nasce la vita. Celabili all'occorrenza, descrivono un paesaggio aperto a numerose prospettive.

Dream Unit: rilassamento e intelletto, camera, guardaroba e video integrato (materiali: cuoio e legno)
Pure Unit: rilassamento e sensazione, cura del corpo (materiali: Corian© e lava)
Flavour Unit: rilassamento e affetto, luogo da sogno con giardino aromatico (materiali: Corian© e acciaio inossidabile)

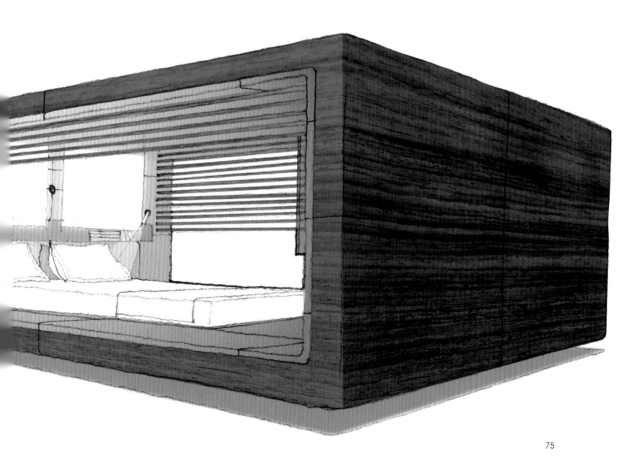

HIP
SPA, BEAUTY & HAIRSTYLING SALON |
NICE, 2002
Surface area: 500 m^2

LANCÔME FLAGSHIPS
STORES & SPA | PARIS, NEW YORK, SHANGHAI,
SEOUL, HONG KONG, 2003-2005
Client: Lancôme, France
Brand Identity

AXOR WATERDREAM
INSTALLATION | MILAN, 2005
Client: Axor / Hansgrohe, Germany

RENAULT MOTOR SHOWS
SHOW STANDS | PARIS, GENEVA,
TOKYO, FRANKFURT, 2000-2005
Client: Renault SA, France
Brand Identity

In agreement with the brand image these installations focus their attention on the individual. It not only propounds the idea of a stand as such but also of a welcoming environment where the visitor can understand the brand as turning towards progress that encapsulates the noble, the innate respect and total well being. It is more a suggested atmosphere than a piece of learned architecture. The site represents an abstract landscape composed of energy rather than matter. The relief of the ground reflects the volume of the ceiling, emphasizing the vitality of the interior.

In Übereinstimmung mit der Herstellermarke setzen diese Installationen das Individuum in den Mittelpunkt. Es wurde nicht einfach ein Stand vorgeschlagen, sondern ein Empfangsuniversum, in dem der Besucher eine Firma erkennt, die sich den edlen Aspekten des Fortschritts, dem Respekt und dem Wohlbefinden verschreibt. Es handelt sich eher um ein suggestives Klima als um eine zweckmäßige Architektur. Der Ort als abstrakte Landschaft, eher aus Energie als aus Materie zusammengefügt. Das Bodenrelief entspricht dem Deckenvolumen, um die Messeevents hervorzuheben.

De acuerdo con la imagen de la marca, estas instalaciones colocan al individuo en el centro de sus preocupaciones. Aquí no se ha propuesto un pabellón sino un universo de acogida donde el visitante puede aprehender una marca dirigida hacia el progreso en lo que tiene de noble, a conocer el respeto y el bienestar. Se trata más de un ambiente sugestivo que de una arquitectura sabia. El lugar es un paisaje abstracto más compuesto de energía que de materia. Al volumen del suelo le responde el volumen del techo para subrrayar los acontecimientos del salón.

A l'image de la marque, ces installations placent l'individu au centre de ses préoccupations. Il n'y est pas proposé un stand mais un univers d'accueil ou le visiteur peux appréhender une marque tournée vers le progrès dans ce qu'il a de noble, à savoir le respect et le bien-être. C'est un climat suggestif plus qu'une architecture savante. Le lieu est un paysage abstrait composé de plus d'énergie que de matière. Au relief du sol répond le volume du plafond pour souligner les événements du salon.

Al pari del marchio, queste installazioni collocano l'individuo al centro delle sue preoccupazioni. Non viene proposto uno stand, ma un universo di accoglienza in cui il visitatore può riconoscere un marchio che si rivolge agli aspetti nobili del progresso, ovvero il rispetto e il benessere. È un ambiente suggestivo più che un'architettura funzionale. Il luogo è un paesaggio astratto composto più da energia che da materia. Al rilievo del terreno corrisponde il volume del soffitto, così da sottolineare gli eventi del salone.

POLTRONA FRAU
SHOWROOM | MILAN, ROME, NEW YORK, 2005
Client: Poltrona Frau, Italy

FURNITURE & OBJECTS

GHOSTHOME
HEAVEN, FRANCE
Seat, 2001

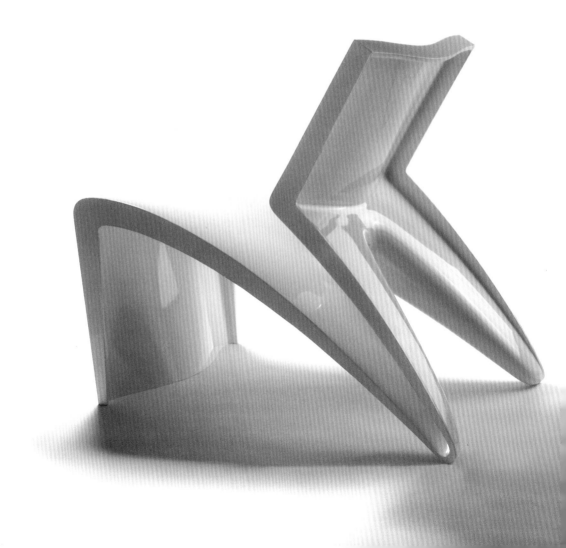

CHUCK
E&Y, JAPAN
Rocking Chair, 1997

VADER
PROTOTYPE, FRANCE
Sofa, 1997

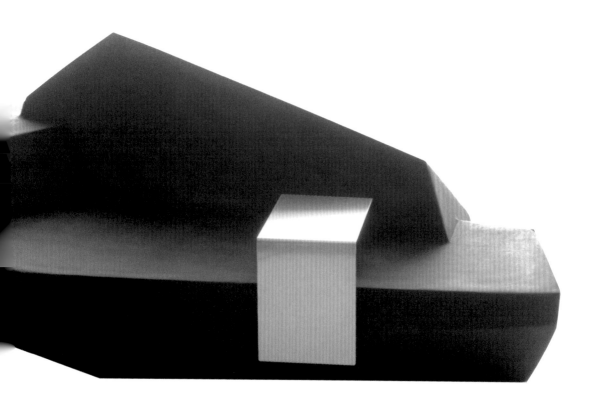

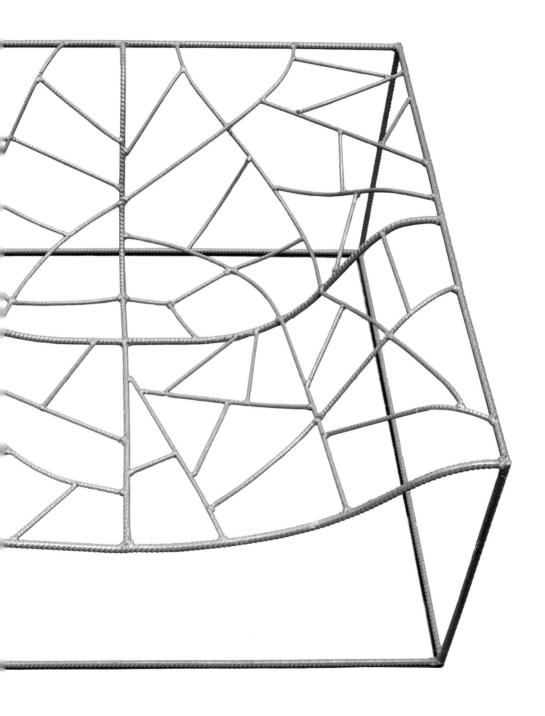

CAO
PROTOTYPE, FRANCE
Seat Sculpture, 1999

O-AZARD
MAGIS, ITALY
Chair, 1998

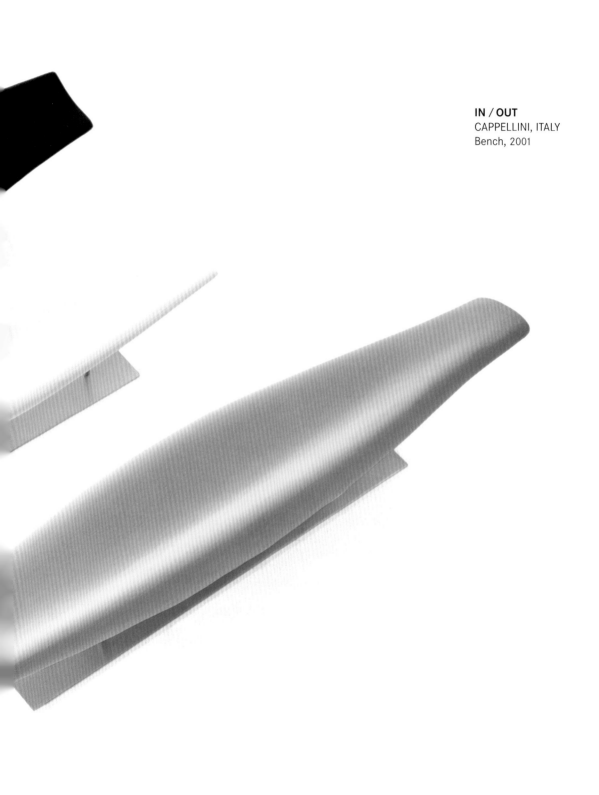

IN / OUT
CAPPELLINI, ITALY
Bench, 2001

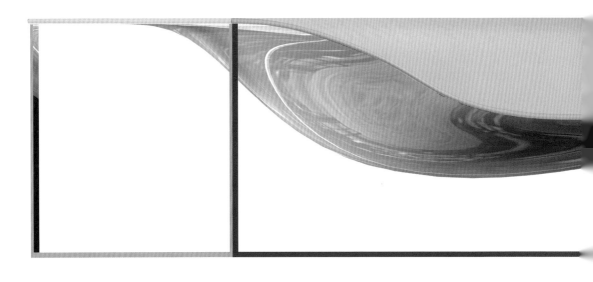

OUTLINE
CAPPELLINI, ITALY
Day Bed, 2001

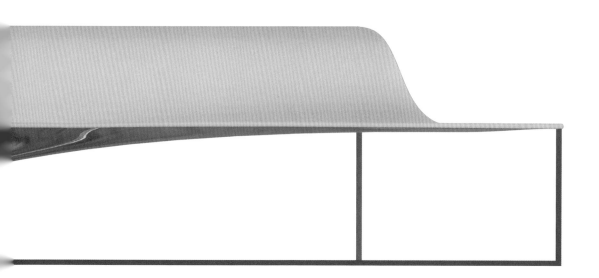

AUCKLAND
CASSINA, ITALY
Armchair, 2004

ASPEN
CASSINA, ITALY
Sofa, 2004

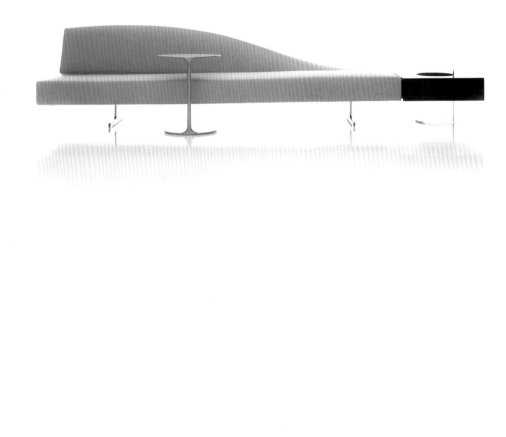

JAZZ
TIME & STYLE, JAPAN
Lounge System, 2005

PEBBLE
PORRO, ITALY
Coffee Table,
Chevet & Stool Collection, 2005

TRUFFLE
PORRO, ITALY
Seat, 2005

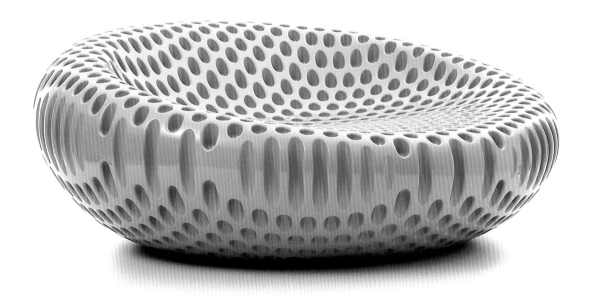

OVERSCALED CANDLES
B&B ITALIA, ITALY
Candles Collection, 2005

DON' DO
POLTRONA FRAU, ITALY
Rocking Chair, 2005

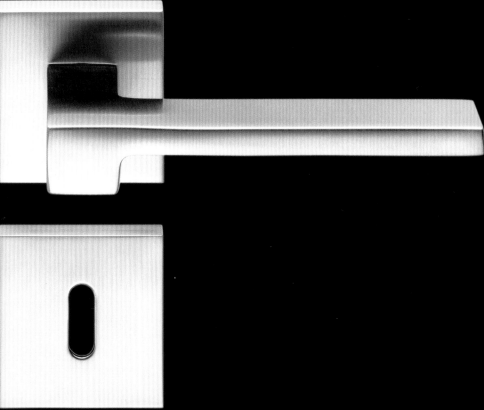

ZELDA
COLOMBO DESIGN, ITALY
Doorhandle, 2004

ASTER X
POLTRONA FRAU, ITALY
Chair, 2005

LIPLA
PORRO, ITALY
Bed, 2005

ASTON
ARPER, ITALY
Lounge Chair, 2006

AKI
TIME & STYLE, JAPAN
Lounge Chair and Ottoman, 2006

MÈN
TIME & STYLE, JAPAN
Lounge Chair, 2006

SYNAPSIS
PORRO, ITALY
Table and Trestle System, 2006

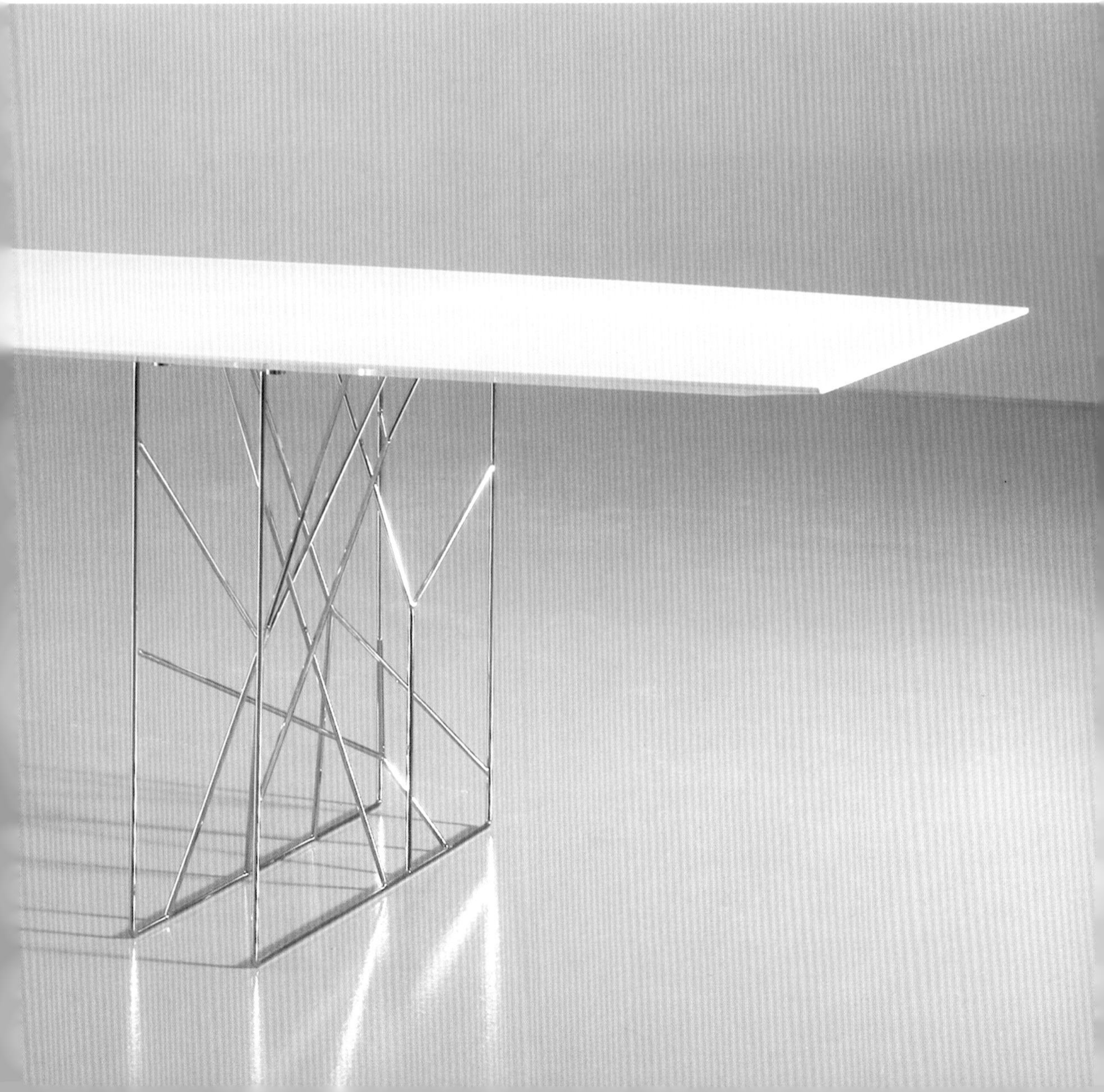

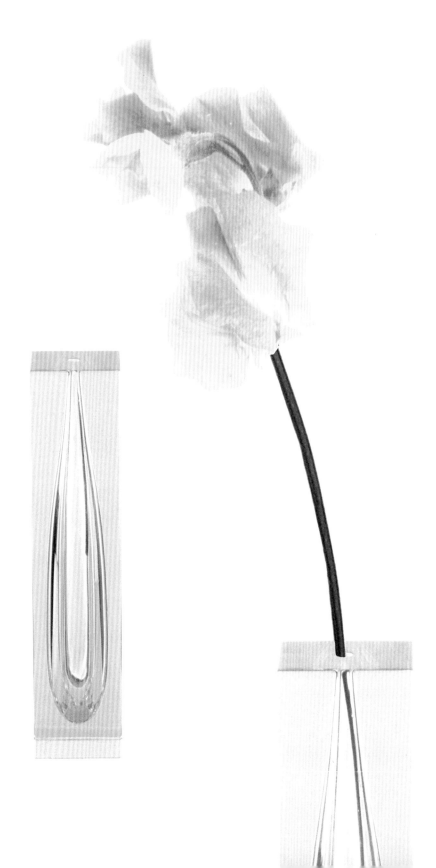

PARADOXE
BACCARAT, FRANCE
Bowl, 1998

PALOMA PICASSO
PALOMA PICASSO, FRANCE
Flask, Female Fragrance, 2002

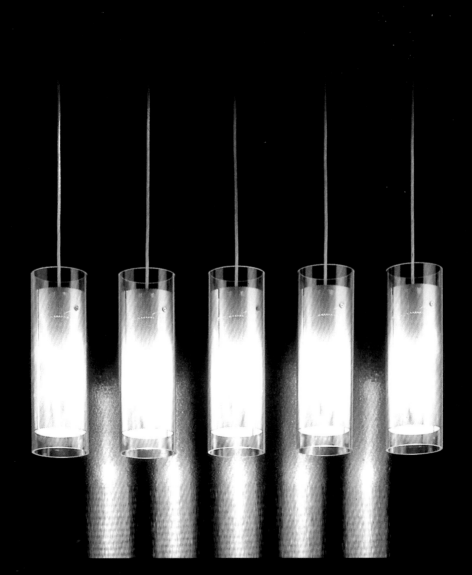

MIROIR 1.2.3
DE VECCHI, ITALY
Mirror, Basket / Table Center, 2002

TRAY
DE VECCHI, ITALY
Table Center, 2002

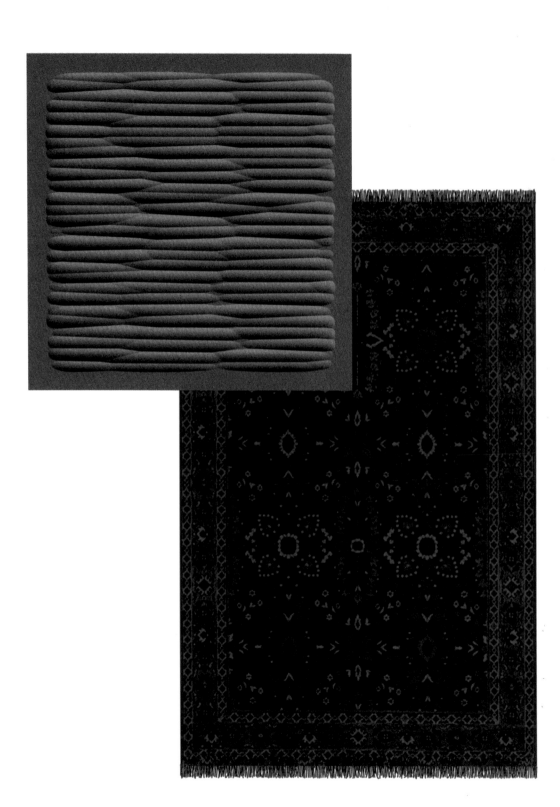

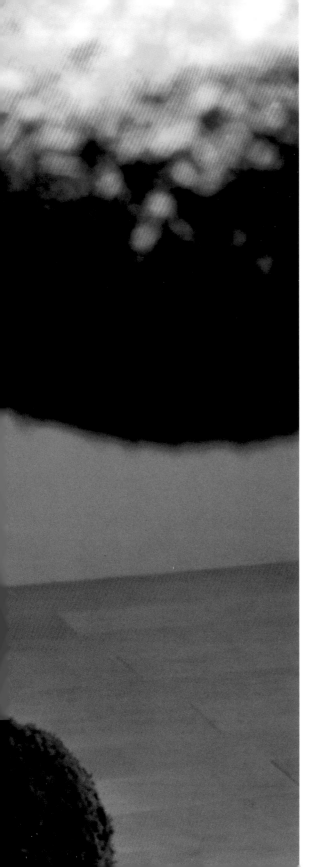

GREEN COLONY
TIME & STYLE, JAPAN
Plant Sculpture, 2002

VENT BLANC
TIME & STYLE, JAPAN
Table Set, 2005

AXOR-MASSAUD
AXOR / HANSGROHE, GERMANY
Faucets Collection,
Bathroom Components
and Accessories, 2005

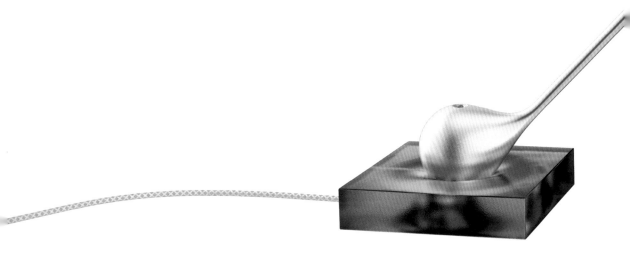

SWING
PROTOTYPE, FRANCE
LED Table & Floor Lamp, 1995

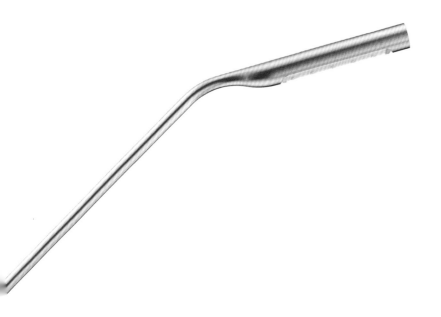

SESA 570
YAMAHA OFF-SHORE, JAPAN
Dry Equi Pressure Submarine, 1992

STAMP RADIO
LEXON, FRANCE
Radio Am / Fm, 1995

LIFT
MIZUNO, JAPAN
Tennis Racket, 1996

BEunique

BE UNIQUE
LE CERCLE, FRANCE
Flask, Male Fragrance, 1998

NESS COLLECTION
BACK, GERMANY
Office Accessories, 2000

NEMO
CACHAREL, FRANCE
Flask, Male Fragrance, 2000

RUNE
PROTOTYPE, FRANCE
Mobile Phone, 2006

MANED CLOUD
PROJECT, FRANCE
Sky Cruiser, 2005

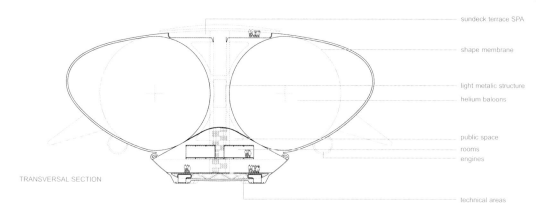

sundeck terrace SPA

shape membrane

light metalic structure
helium baloons

public space
rooms
engines

technical areas

TRANSVERSAL SECTION

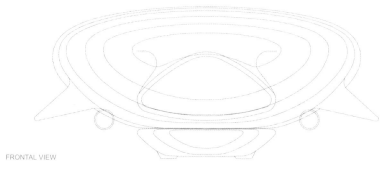

FRONTAL VIEW

TERRACE LEVEL

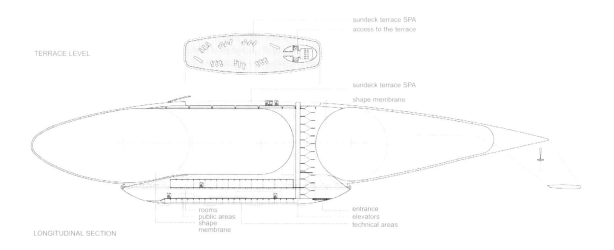

sundeck terrace SPA
access to the terrace

sundeck terrace SPA
shape membrane

rooms
public areas
shape
membrane

entrance
elevators
technical areas

LONGITUDINAL SECTION

INDEX

STUDIO MASSAUD
7, rue Tolain, F-75020 Paris
P + 33 (0)1 40 09 54 14
F + 33 (0)1 40 09 08 16
studio@massaud.com
www.massaud.com

Jean-Marie Massaud

Born in Toulouse (France) in 1966, Jean-Marie Massaud is first of all a child fascinated by the scientific imagery, who dreams of becoming an inventor.

He graduates from enScI (Paris) in 1990 and starts collaborating with Marc Berthier.

In 2000, he founds Studio Massaud together with Daniel Pouzet and expands his expertise to architecture.

Honored with numerous prizes and awards, some of his creations can be found among the collections of the great museums of art and design around the world (in Amsterdam, Chicago, Lisbon, London, Paris and Zurich).

In 2005, an exclusive exhibition of his work took place in Tokyo.

Daniel Pouzet

Daniel Pouzet was born in Bucharest (Romania) in 1967.

He graduates from the Ion Mincu Architecture School (Bucharest) and UP4 (Charenton-Paris) in 1996.
Top of his year, he partakes in many national competitions.

His project for a Third Airport in Paris is awarded by the French Iron Structures Union.

In 1997, he receives an honor from the Society of Fine Arts. While teaching at the UP4 School of Architecture (Charenton-Paris), he collaborates with Philippe STARCK until 2002, taking part in various large-scale projects in France, the UK and the US.

References

Design

Armani

Baccarat

Cacharel

Cappellini

Cassina

De Vecchi

Dornbracht

E & Y

Habitat

Lancôme

Lanvin

Lexon

Liv'It

Ligne Roset

Magis

Mazzega

Mizuno

Offect

Paloma Picasso

Poltrona Frau

Tronconi

Yamaha Offshore

Yves Saint Laurent

Interior Design

Chanel

EMI, London

HIP Spa, Nice

Lancôme, stores & spas

Nike

Prost

Sephora

The Modern Object

Brand Architectural Identities

Lancôme

Poltrona Frau

Renault

Sephora

Architecture

Omnilife Condominium Towers, Guadalajara, Mexico

Football Stadium, Guadalajara, Mexico

Hotel & Spa Puerto, Vallarta, Mexico

TRIB' TRIBE HUT Condominium Towers, TriBeCa, NYC, USA

Town & Shelter

Mama Shelter Hotel, Boulogne-Billancourt, France

Resort Hotel, Palm Springs, California, USA

Awards & Distinctions

2006	IF Product – Forum Prize – AXOR collection
2005	Designer of the Year / ELLE DECO, France
	Best Eco Design (Human Nature), Design Tide / AP Bank, Tokyo
2004	APCI Observeur du Design, Paris (O'Azard chair & Ness Collection)
2002	Talents du Luxe, Paris
2001	Etoiles APCI Observeur du Design (Ness Collection & Séphora Blanc), France
2000	Arests Best – Best Perfume Bottle (Nemo Cacharel), Norway
1999	Nombre d'Or (Salon du Meuble in Paris), France
1996	Chair of the Year (Promosedia dell'Anno), Italy
	FORM Prize, Germany
	Grand Prix de la Presse Internationale et de la critique du meuble contemporain
	First Prize Maquill'Art, Paris
1995	VIA Carte Blanche, Paris
1995-98	Compasso d'Oro: 3 Selections, Italy
1994-96	3 Top Ten, Italy

Photocredits

© 2007 daab
cologne london new york

published and distributed worldwide by
daab gmbh
friesenstr. 50
d - 50670 köln

p +49 - 221 - 913 927 0
f +49 - 221 - 913 927 20

mail@daab-online.com
www.daab-online.com

publisher ralf daab
rdaab@daab-online.com

creative director feyyaz
mail@feyyaz.com

layout alexandra zöller
a.zoeller@snafu.de

editorial project by caroline klein
caroline_klein@hotmail.com

text by studio massaud
introduction by caroline klein

english translation mechthild barth, caroline klein, studio massaud
german translation caroline klein
spanish translation concepción dueso
french translation inge klein-kelling
italian translation laura santi, alessandro randolfi
translations by durante & zoratti, cologne and caroline klein, milan
copy editing by caroline klein, milan and durante & zoratti, cologne

litho licht & tiefe, berlin

printed in czech republic
www.graspo.com

isbn   978 - 3 - 937718 - 88 - 0